THIS BOOK BELONGS TO:

....

....

....

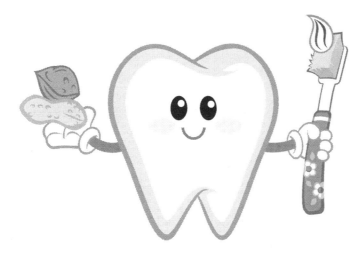

Free Goodies! Visit Our Website : PodTreasury.com

WEEK OF ....

TOOTH BRUSH CHART

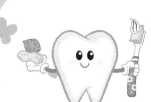

	MORNING	NIGHT
Monday	⬭	⬭
Tuesday	⬭	⬭
Wednesday	⬭	⬭
Thursday	⬭	⬭
Friday	⬭	⬭
Saturday	⬭	⬭
Sunday	⬭	⬭

 REWARDS

WEEK OF ....

TOOTH BRUSH CHART

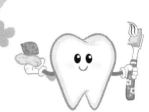

	MORNING	NIGHT
Monday		
Tuesday		
Wednesday		
Thursday		
Friday		
Saturday		
Sunday		

 REWARDS

WEEK OF ....

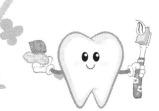

TOOTH BRUSH
CHART

	MORNING	NIGHT
Monday	🦷	🦷
Tuesday	🦷	🦷
Wednesday	🦷	🦷
Thursday	🦷	🦷
Friday	🦷	🦷
Saturday	🦷	🦷
Sunday	🦷	🦷

 REWARDS

WEEK OF ....

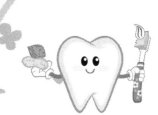 ## TOOTH BRUSH CHART

	MORNING	NIGHT
Monday	🦷	🦷
Tuesday	🦷	🦷
Wednesday	🦷	🦷
Thursday	🦷	🦷
Friday	🦷	🦷
Saturday	🦷	🦷
Sunday	🦷	🦷

 REWARDS

WEEK OF ....

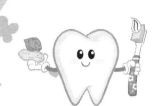

TOOTH BRUSH CHART

	MORNING	NIGHT
Monday	◯	◯
Tuesday	◯	◯
Wednesday	◯	◯
Thursday	◯	◯
Friday	◯	◯
Saturday	◯	◯
Sunday	◯	◯

 REWARDS

WEEK OF ....

TOOTH BRUSH CHART

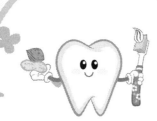

	MORNING	NIGHT
Monday		
Tuesday		
Wednesday		
Thursday		
Friday		
Saturday		
Sunday		

 REWARDS

WEEK OF ....

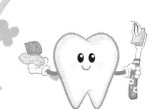

TOOTH BRUSH CHART

	MORNING	NIGHT
Monday		
Tuesday		
Wednesday		
Thursday		
Friday		
Saturday		
Sunday		

 REWARDS

WEEK OF ....

TOOTH BRUSH CHART

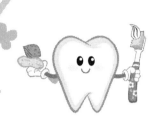

	MORNING	NIGHT
Monday	🦷	🦷
Tuesday	🦷	🦷
Wednesday	🦷	🦷
Thursday	🦷	🦷
Friday	🦷	🦷
Saturday	🦷	🦷
Sunday	🦷	🦷

 REWARDS

WEEK OF ....

TOOTH BRUSH CHART

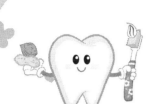

	MORNING	NIGHT
Monday	🦷	🦷
Tuesday	🦷	🦷
Wednesday	🦷	🦷
Thursday	🦷	🦷
Friday	🦷	🦷
Saturday	🦷	🦷
Sunday	🦷	🦷

 REWARDS

WEEK OF ....

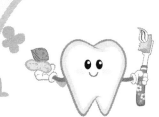

TOOTH BRUSH CHART

	MORNING	NIGHT
Monday		
Tuesday		
Wednesday		
Thursday		
Friday		
Saturday		
Sunday		

 REWARDS

WEEK OF ....

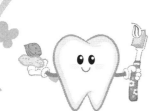

TOOTH BRUSH CHART

	MORNING	NIGHT
Monday	🦷	🦷
Tuesday	🦷	🦷
Wednesday	🦷	🦷
Thursday	🦷	🦷
Friday	🦷	🦷
Saturday	🦷	🦷
Sunday	🦷	🦷

 REWARDS

WEEK OF ....

TOOTH BRUSH CHART

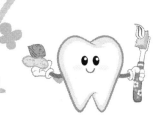

	MORNING	NIGHT
Monday	♡	♡
Tuesday	♡	♡
Wednesday	♡	♡
Thursday	♡	♡
Friday	♡	♡
Saturday	♡	♡
Sunday	♡	♡

 REWARDS

WEEK OF ....

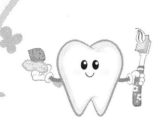

TOOTH BRUSH
CHART

	MORNING	NIGHT
Monday	🦷	🦷
Tuesday	🦷	🦷
Wednesday	🦷	🦷
Thursday	🦷	🦷
Friday	🦷	🦷
Saturday	🦷	🦷
Sunday	🦷	🦷

 REWARDS

WEEK OF ....

TOOTH BRUSH CHART

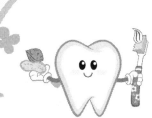

	MORNING	NIGHT
Monday	♡	♡
Tuesday	♡	♡
Wednesday	♡	♡
Thursday	♡	♡
Friday	♡	♡
Saturday	♡	♡
Sunday	♡	♡

 REWARDS

WEEK OF ....

TOOTH BRUSH CHART

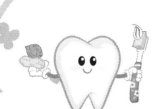

	MORNING	NIGHT
Monday	🦷	🦷
Tuesday	🦷	🦷
Wednesday	🦷	🦷
Thursday	🦷	🦷
Friday	🦷	🦷
Saturday	🦷	🦷
Sunday	🦷	🦷

 REWARDS

WEEK OF ....

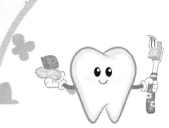

TOOTH BRUSH CHART

	MORNING	NIGHT
Monday	🦷	🦷
Tuesday	🦷	🦷
Wednesday	🦷	🦷
Thursday	🦷	🦷
Friday	🦷	🦷
Saturday	🦷	🦷
Sunday	🦷	🦷

 REWARDS

20

WEEK OF ....

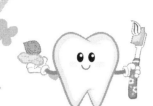

TOOTH BRUSH CHART

	MORNING	NIGHT
Monday		
Tuesday		
Wednesday		
Thursday		
Friday		
Saturday		
Sunday		

 REWARDS

WEEK OF ....

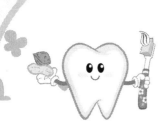

TOOTH BRUSH CHART

	MORNING	NIGHT
Monday	♢	♢
Tuesday	♢	♢
Wednesday	♢	♢
Thursday	♢	♢
Friday	♢	♢
Saturday	♢	♢
Sunday	♢	♢

 REWARDS

WEEK OF ....

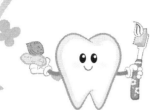

TOOTH BRUSH CHART

	MORNING	NIGHT
Monday	♡	♡
Tuesday	♡	♡
Wednesday	♡	♡
Thursday	♡	♡
Friday	♡	♡
Saturday	♡	♡
Sunday	♡	♡

 REWARDS

WEEK OF ....

TOOTH BRUSH CHART

	MORNING	NIGHT
Monday	♡	♡
Tuesday	♡	♡
Wednesday	♡	♡
Thursday	♡	♡
Friday	♡	♡
Saturday	♡	♡
Sunday	♡	♡

 REWARDS

WEEK OF ....

TOOTH BRUSH CHART

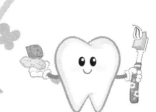

	MORNING	NIGHT
Monday	♡	♡
Tuesday	♡	♡
Wednesday	♡	♡
Thursday	♡	♡
Friday	♡	♡
Saturday	♡	♡
Sunday	♡	♡

 REWARDS

WEEK OF ....

TOOTH BRUSH CHART

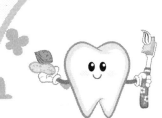

	MORNING	NIGHT
Monday		
Tuesday		
Wednesday		
Thursday		
Friday		
Saturday		
Sunday		

 REWARDS

WEEK OF ....

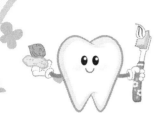

TOOTH BRUSH CHART

	MORNING	NIGHT
Monday	⬡	⬡
Tuesday	⬡	⬡
Wednesday	⬡	⬡
Thursday	⬡	⬡
Friday	⬡	⬡
Saturday	⬡	⬡
Sunday	⬡	⬡

 REWARDS

WEK OF ....

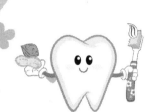

TOOTH BRUSH
CHART

	MORNING	NIGHT
Monday	🦷	🦷
Tuesday	🦷	🦷
Wednesday	🦷	🦷
Thursday	🦷	🦷
Friday	🦷	🦷
Saturday	🦷	🦷
Sunday	🦷	🦷

 REWARDS

WEEK OF ....

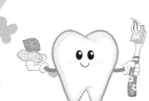

TOOTH BRUSH CHART

	MORNING	NIGHT
Monday		
Tuesday		
Wednesday		
Thursday		
Friday		
Saturday		
Sunday		

 REWARDS

WEEK OF ....

TOOTH BRUSH CHART

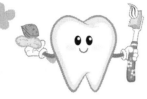

	MORNING	NIGHT
Monday		
Tuesday		
Wednesday		
Thursday		
Friday		
Saturday		
Sunday		

 REWARDS

WEEK OF ....

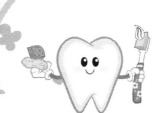

TOOTH BRUSH CHART

	MORNING	NIGHT
Monday		
Tuesday		
Wednesday		
Thursday		
Friday		
Saturday		
Sunday		

 REWARDS

WEEK OF ....

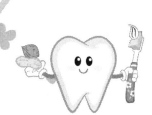

TOOTH BRUSH CHART

	MORNING	NIGHT
Monday		
Tuesday		
Wednesday		
Thursday		
Friday		
Saturday		
Sunday		

 REWARDS

WEEK OF ....

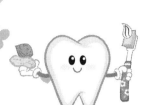

TOOTH BRUSH CHART

	MORNING	NIGHT
Monday		
Tuesday		
Wednesday		
Thursday		
Friday		
Saturday		
Sunday		

 REWARDS

WEEK OF ....

TOOTH BRUSH CHART

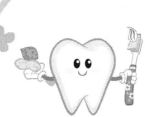

MORNING NIGHT

	Morning	Night
Monday		
Tuesday		
Wednesday		
Thursday		
Friday		
Saturday		
Sunday		

 REWARDS

WEEK OF ....

TOOTH BRUSH CHART

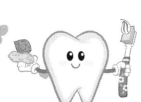

	MORNING	NIGHT
Monday		
Tuesday		
Wednesday		
Thursday		
Friday		
Saturday		
Sunday		

 REWARDS

WEEK OF ....

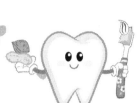

TOOTH BRUSH CHART

	MORNING	NIGHT
Monday		
Tuesday		
Wednesday		
Thursday		
Friday		
Saturday		
Sunday		

 REWARDS

WEEK OF ....

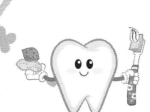

TOOTH BRUSH
CHART

MORNING   NIGHT

Monday

Tuesday

Wednesday

Thursday

Friday

Saturday

Sunday

 REWARDS

WEEK OF ....

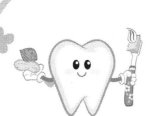

TOOTH BRUSH
CHART

MORNING　　　NIGHT

Monday

Tuesday

Wednesday

Thursday

Friday

Saturday

Sunday

 REWARDS

WEEK OF ....

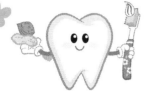

TOOTH BRUSH CHART

	MORNING	NIGHT
Monday	🦷	🦷
Tuesday	🦷	🦷
Wednesday	🦷	🦷
Thursday	🦷	🦷
Friday	🦷	🦷
Saturday	🦷	🦷
Sunday	🦷	🦷

 REWARDS

WEEK OF ....

TOOTH BRUSH CHART

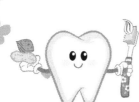

	MORNING	NIGHT
Monday	🦷	🦷
Tuesday	🦷	🦷
Wednesday	🦷	🦷
Thursday	🦷	🦷
Friday	🦷	🦷
Saturday	🦷	🦷
Sunday	🦷	🦷

 REWARDS

WEEK OF ....

TOOTH BRUSH CHART

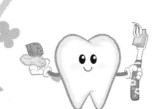

	MORNING	NIGHT
Monday		
Tuesday		
Wednesday		
Thursday		
Friday		
Saturday		
Sunday		

 REWARDS

WEEK OF ....

TOOTH BRUSH CHART

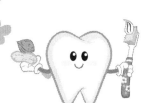

	MORNING	NIGHT
Monday		
Tuesday		
Wednesday		
Thursday		
Friday		
Saturday		
Sunday		

 REWARDS

WEEK OF ....

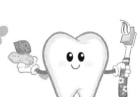 TOOTH BRUSH CHART

	MORNING	NIGHT
Monday		
Tuesday		
Wednesday		
Thursday		
Friday		
Saturday		
Sunday		

 REWARDS

WEEK OF ....

TOOTH BRUSH CHART

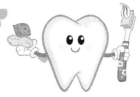

	MORNING	NIGHT
Monday		
Tuesday		
Wednesday		
Thursday		
Friday		
Saturday		
Sunday		

 REWARDS

WEEK OF ....

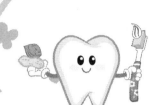

TOOTH BRUSH CHART

	MORNING	NIGHT
Monday	♡	♡
Tuesday	♡	♡
Wednesday	♡	♡
Thursday	♡	♡
Friday	♡	♡
Saturday	♡	♡
Sunday	♡	♡

 REWARDS

WEEK OF ....

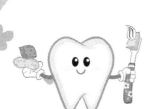 

MORNING   NIGHT

Monday

Tuesday

Wednesday

Thursday

Friday

Saturday

Sunday

 REWARDS

WEEK OF ....

TOOTH BRUSH CHART

	MORNING	NIGHT
Monday		
Tuesday		
Wednesday		
Thursday		
Friday		
Saturday		
Sunday		

 REWARDS

WEEK OF ....

TOOTH BRUSH CHART

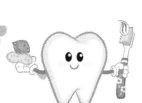

	MORNING	NIGHT
Monday		
Tuesday		
Wednesday		
Thursday		
Friday		
Saturday		
Sunday		

 REWARDS

WEEK OF ....

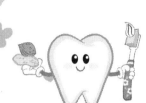

TOOTH BRUSH CHART

	MORNING	NIGHT
Monday		
Tuesday		
Wednesday		
Thursday		
Friday		
Saturday		
Sunday		

 REWARDS

WEEK OF ....

TOOTH BRUSH CHART

	MORNING	NIGHT
Monday		
Tuesday		
Wednesday		
Thursday		
Friday		
Saturday		
Sunday		

 REWARDS

WEEK OF ....

TOOTH BRUSH
CHART

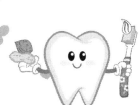

	MORNING	NIGHT
Monday		
Tuesday		
Wednesday		
Thursday		
Friday		
Saturday		
Sunday		

 REWARDS

WEEK OF ....

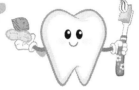

TOOTH BRUSH CHART

	MORNING	NIGHT
Monday		
Tuesday		
Wednesday		
Thursday		
Friday		
Saturday		
Sunday		

 REWARDS

WEEK OF ....

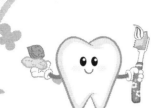 # TOOTH BRUSH CHART

	MORNING	NIGHT
Monday		
Tuesday		
Wednesday		
Thursday		
Friday		
Saturday		
Sunday		

 REWARDS

WEEK OF ....

TOOTH BRUSH CHART

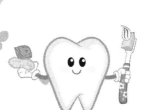

	MORNING	NIGHT
Monday		
Tuesday		
Wednesday		
Thursday		
Friday		
Saturday		
Sunday		

 REWARDS

WEEK OF ....

TOOTH BRUSH CHART

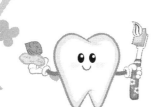

	MORNING	NIGHT
Monday	🦷	🦷
Tuesday	🦷	🦷
Wednesday	🦷	🦷
Thursday	🦷	🦷
Friday	🦷	🦷
Saturday	🦷	🦷
Sunday	🦷	🦷

 REWARDS

WEEK OF ....

TOOTH BRUSH CHART

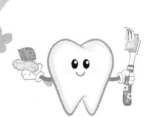

	MORNING	NIGHT
Monday		
Tuesday		
Wednesday		
Thursday		
Friday		
Saturday		
Sunday		

 REWARDS

Manufactured by Amazon.ca
Bolton, ON

37204529R00033